What Allah says about Anger Management and Using Intoxicants!

Although anger is a natural feeling it can have negative effects on those who allow it to control them, and adverse effects on those around them. Uncontrolled anger is one of the tools of Satan, and it can lead to many evils and tragedies. For this reason Islam has a great deal to say about the emotion of anger.

Because anger is often associated with 'fight or flight responses', it is often difficult to separate an action done in self-defense, to protect properties or families, from one that is done out of uncontrolled rage. It is ok to feel anger. However, it is not acceptable when a person allows it to overtake him, and drives him to act in an unacceptable way; sometimes even leading to chaos and murder. The story of an event in the life of one of Prophet Muhammad's (saws) companions, his son-in-law Ali, demonstrates the difference.

Prophet Muhammed's (saws) son in law, Ali was once fighting in a war, when the leader of the non-Muslim army attacked him. During the confrontation, Ali managed to overcome him, and was on the verge of killing him, when his opponent spat in Ali's face. Ali immediately stepped back and left the man alone. The man said, "You could have killed me, why did you stop? Ali answered, "I have no personal hatred toward you. I was fighting you because of your disbelief in, and rebellion against Allah. If I had killed you after you spat in my face, it would have been because of my personal anger, and desire for revenge, which I do not wish to take."

It has been said: "Protect yourself from anger for its beginning is insanity and its end is remorse."

The Prophet (saws) once asked his Companions, "Whom among you do you consider a strong man?" They replied, "The one who can defeat so-and-so in a wrestling match." He said, "That is not so. A strong man is the one who can control himself when he is angry."

As always if a person is unsure about how to act in any situation he need only look to Prophet Muhammad (saws), or our righteous predecessors to find the best way to act. Prophet Muhammad (saws) was known as a man who could, and would, even under desperate circumstances control his anger. One day the Prophet (saws) was attacked by a Bedouin, who roughly seized him by the neck part of his cloak. The marks left on his neck could be seen by his companions. The Bedouin demanded Prophet Muhammad (saws) give him some of the wealth. The Prophet (saws) turned to him and smiled, then ordered that he (the Bedouin) should be given something agreeable to him.

We can also follow the example of the Prophet (saws) by using our anger for the sake of Allah, when our rights are violated. This is the kind of controlled anger, which is praiseworthy. Prophet Muhammad (saws) became angry when he was told about the imam who was upsetting people in the prayer by making it too long, and when he saw a curtain with pictures of live creatures, and when he was asked questions that he disliked. However his anger was purely for the sake of Allah, he did not fly off the handle, rant and rave, or make people fear to be in his presence.

When Prophet Mohammad (saws) became angry due to someone's incorrect actions or their words, he never expressed it with his hand, and used only mild words. In fact those that did not know him well did not even suspect that he was angry. His companions however, knew that he was angry, by just looking at him. His face would turn red and his forehead would bead with sweat. However, rather than expressing his anger openly he would be quiet, using those first few moments to control himself.

Controlling anger is a sign of righteousness. A righteous person is promised Paradise. One of the characteristics of righteousness is being able to control anger. Allah says: "And march forth in the way (which leads to) forgiveness from your Lord, and for Paradise as wide as the heavens and the earth, is prepared for the pious. Those who spend (in Allah's Cause) in prosperity, and in adversity. Who repress anger, and who pardon the people. Verily, Allah loves the good-doers."(3 Al i Imran:133-134)

Allah also says: "So whatever you have been given is but (a passing) enjoyment, for this worldly life. However, that which is with Allah, Paradise, is better and more lasting for those who believe, and put their trust in their Lord. And those who avoid the greater sins, and illegal sexual intercourse, and when they are angry, they forgive." (42 Ash-Shura:36 & 37)

Anger is a very natural human emotion. It is also very powerful, and can vary in intensity from mild irritation, to intense fury and rage. The latter can be destructive. It can rage through a person, creating a desire for revenge, and pushing a person to strike out at the object of his anger. Because it is natural it is impossible for a person to avoid it completely. It is however possible to understand anger, and thus control it.

When a person becomes angry, whether as a result of a stimulus or not, he has the choice to control his anger by responding to it in a way sanctioned by the Qur'an, and the traditions of Prophet Muhammad (saws), or, he could give in to the wave of emotion, and behave in a way that displeases Allah, but delights Satan.

In the era when it appears that Islam is being belittled all over the globe many Muslims are letting their anger get the better of them. Yes, it hurts to have our religion, and our beloved Prophet (saws) abused and vilified. However, as believers, we should not let our emotions dictate our actions. Actions are to be based on divine knowledge, and wisdom. We cannot completely stop those who tarnish Islam with their lies and deception, but we can control ourselves, educate the masses, and take other positive steps legislated by Islam.

In part 2 we will look at examples of how to behave when angry, taken from the Qur'an and the traditions of Prophet Muhammad (saws).

Allah says: "Whatever you have been given, is merely a provision for the transitory life of this world, and that which is with Allah is better, as well as, more lasting. That is for those who have believed and put their trust in their Lord, and Who refrain from gross sins and indecencies. Who, when they are angry, forgive. Who, obey their Lord, establish the Prayer, and conduct their affairs by mutual consultation. Who spend out of what We have given them as sustenance. Who, when they are oppressed, help and defend themselves. The recompense of evil is a like evil, then whoever pardons, and seeks reconcilement, his reward is with Allah. Allah does not like the wrongdoers. Those who avenge themselves after they have been wronged, cannot be held blameworthy, for blameworthy indeed are those who oppress others and commit excesses in the land, without any right. For such people there is a painful torment. However, the one who practices patience and is forgiving, these indeed are works of great courage, and resolution." [42 Ash-Shura:36-43]

As it relates to wealth, "It is not a thing which man should rejoice at. Whatever worldly wealth a person has in his possession, he has it only for a short time. He uses it for a few years, and then leaves the world empty-handed. Then, although the amount of the wealth may be very high, on the books, practically speaking only a fraction of it is used by the man himself. To rejoice at such wealth, does not behoove a man who understands the truth about himself, about his wealth and this world itself." That means it is not eternal nor everlasting.

Trust (tawakkul) in Allah has been regarded as a demand of the faith and a necessary characteristic for success in the Hereafter. Tawakkul means:

(1) That man should have full confidence in the guidance of Allah, and understand that knowledge of the truth, the principles of morality, the boundaries of the lawful and unlawful, and the rules and regulations of this life, that Allah has ordered, are based on the truth, and in following them alone lies man's well being, and

(2) man should not place reliance on his own powers and abilities, nor his own means and resources, plans and schemes, nor the help of others than Allah. Instead, he should keep deeply impressed in his mind the fact that his success in everything, here and in the Hereafter, actually depends on the help and support of Allah. That he can become worthy of Allah's help, and support only if he works with the object of winning Allah's approval, within the boundaries prescribed by Allah

(3) man should have complete faith in the promises that Allah has made with those who adopt the way of faith and righteousness. Who work in the cause of the truth, instead of

falsehood. Who have faith in the same promises, and discard all benefits, gains and pleasures that seem to accrue from following the way of falsehood. Who endure all losses, hardships and deprivations, that may become his lot, on account of following the truth steadfastly. From this explanation of the meaning of tawakkul it becomes obvious how deeply it is related with the faith, and why those wonderful results that have been promised to the believers who practice tawakkul, cannot be obtained from empty affirmation of the faith.

The Believers are not angry and crazy, but are temperate and cool minded. They are not revengeful, but resist the temptation, and are forgiving by nature. If ever they feel angry at something they control their rage. This characteristic is the best of man's qualities.

According to Aishah, "The Holy Messenger of Allah (saws) never avenged himself, or anybody. However, when a thing, ordered to be held sacred by Allah was desecrated, he would mete out the punishment." (Bukhari, Muslim)

One of the best characteristics of the believers is that their tender heartedness, and forgiving nature is not the result of any weakness. They have not been taught to live humbly, and meekly like the hermits and monks. Their nobility demands that when they are victors, they forgive the errors of the conquered. When they possess the power, they avoid vengefulness, and when a weak, or subdued person happens to commit a mistake they overlook it.

When a powerful person, drunk with authority, commits violence against them, they resist, and fight him with all their might. A believer is never cowed by a wicked person, nor bows to an arrogant man. For such people he proves to be a hard nut, which breaks the teeth of those who try to break it.

* The first fundamental principle, which must be borne in mind is the role retaliation plays in anger. The right limit of retaliation is, that one should return the same sort of ill treatment, that one has received. One has no right to return a greater ill treatment.

* The second principle, although it is permissible to retaliate against the one who has committed a violence, forgiving can be more conducive to reconcilement. Pardoning is better, for the sake of reconcilement, than retaliation. Since man pardons the other by suppressing his own feelings, Allah says that the reward of such a one is with Him. For he has suppressed his own self, for the sake of reforming the evil-doers.

* The third principle about retaliation is this: One should not become a wrongdoer, oneself, in the process of avenging a wrong done by another. It is not permissible to do a greater wrong in retaliation for the wrong done. For example, if a person slaps another the other can return only one slap. He cannot shower blows and kicks all over the person. Likewise, it is not right to commit a sin, in retaliation for a sin.

For example, if a wicked man has killed the son of someone, it is not right to go and kill the son of the one who killed your son. Or, if a mean person has violated the chastity of a person's sister or daughter, it is not lawful for him to commit rape on the sister, or daughter of the one who did it to your loved one.

One should note that the qualities of the believers that have been mentioned in these verses, really existed in the lives of the Holy Prophet (saws) and his Companions, and the disbelievers of Mecca were their eye witnesses. Thus, Allah has, in fact, told the disbelievers "The real wealth is not the provisions, that you have received during the transitory life of this world, and are bursting with pride of it. The real wealth are the morals and characteristics, which the believers from your own society have developed by accepting the guidance given in the Qur'an."

Allah says: "O Believers, give up the devouring of interest by doubling and redoubling it, and fear Allah, it is expected that you will achieve (true) success. Guard yourselves against that Fire, which has been prepared for the disbelievers. Obey Allah and His Messenger. It is expected that you will be shown mercy. Hasten to follow the path that leads to forgiveness from your Lord, and to the Garden, which is as vast as the heavens and the earth. It has been prepared for those pious people who spend their wealth freely in the way of Allah, both in prosperity, and in adversity. Who control their rage and forgive other people. Allah likes such good people very much, who, if ever they commit a base deed, or wrong their own soul by the commission of a sin, remember Allah instantly and ask for forgiveness from Him, for their shortcomings. For who, but Allah, can forgive sins? Who do not knowingly persist in the wrongs they did. These will be rewarded with forgiveness from Allah, and with Gardens beneath which canals flow. They will reside therein forever, and how excellent is the reward of those who do good deeds." [3 Al-I-Imran:130-136]

The devouring of interest had created extreme greed, and selfishness in those who took interest. Hatred, anger, and jealousy were created in those who had to pay it. Therefore, Allah has condemned, and prohibited interest and prescribed charity as an antidote to it. It is obvious that Paradise has been reserved for those who practice charity and spend generously. Not for those greedy persons who practice money lending on interest.

Allah says: "(O Messenger,) it is a great mercy of Allah that you are very gentle, and lenient towards them. Had you been harsh and hard hearted, they all would have broken away from you. Pardon them and implore Allah to forgive them, and take counsel with them, in the conduct of the affairs. Then, when once you make up your mind (to do a thing), trust in Allah (and do it). Allah likes those who trust in Him in whatever they do." [3 Al i Imran: 159]

It has been said: "Anger is the key (that opens the door) to all kinds of vices."

Anger is able to destroy lives and relationships, and Prophet Muhammad (saws) called it a hot coal on the heart of a descendant of Adam. There is no fool proof way to completely eliminate anger, because it is a natural human emotion. Islam however gives us many examples of how to control anger, and how to channel it into acceptable actions.

There are also distinct advantages to following the guidelines set out in Islam. It pleases Allah, and the person controlling their anger is rewarded.

The Prophet (saws) said, "If anyone suppresses anger when he is in a position to give vent to it, Allah, the exalted, will call him on the Day of Resurrection and ask him to choose from the rewards offered." He also said, "No one has swallowed back anything more excellent in the sight of Allah, seeking to please Allah, who is Great and Glorious, than anger."

Once a man came to Prophet Mohammad (saws) and said, "Messenger of Allah, teach me some words which I can live by. Do not make them too much for me, in case I forget." He said, "Do not be angry." In the traditions of the Prophet (saws) we are able to find many instances of how to behave when anger threatens to engulf us, or burst out. He said, "If one of you becomes angry while standing he should sit down. If the anger leaves him, well and good, otherwise he should lie down."

The Prophet (saws) also advised us that performing ablution was an acceptable method of anger management. He said, "Anger comes from Satan, Satan was created from fire, and fire is extinguished with water. So, when any of you is angry, he should perform ablution."

In addition, the Prophet Muhammad (saws) suggested that when angry a believer could try other methods to rid himself from the influence of Satan. He once advised a man who was angry and fighting, to seek refuge in Allah from the influence of Satan.

Prophet Muhammad (saws) said to his companions, "I know words that if he were to say them his anger would go away, if he said, I seek refuge with Allah from Satan, what he feels would go away."

Imam Ahmad recorded that Prophet Muhammad (saws) also advised that "If any of you becomes angry, let him keep silent." If a person is trying to be silent, it will obviously restrict his ability to fight, or speak obscenities and harsh words.

In another tradition Prophet Muhammad (saws) offered a sequence of actions to defuse anger. "If any of you becomes angry and he is standing, let him sit down, so his anger will go away. If it does not go away, let him lie down."

Thus we find that Islam offers a person several ways to control the very natural emotion of anger. To begin with, a person should change his position. For example, if one is standing he should sit down; if he is already sitting he should lie down. An angry person could make ablution, and offer two or more extra units of prayer. Or, he could seek refuge in Allah from the angry effects Satan has over him, and finally he could try to focus on the rewards Allah offers those who are patient, merciful and inclined to forgive rather than hold a grudge.

Allah defines righteous people as, "Those who spend (in Allah's Cause) in prosperity and in adversity, who repress anger, and who pardon the people. Verily, Allah loves the good doers." [3 Al-i-Imran:134].

Prophet Muhammad (saws) himself demonstrated enormous restraint and patience when he was insulted, belittled and beaten. As his beloved wife Aisha said, His character was (a reflection of) the Quran.

At a very difficult time in his life Prophet Muhammad (saws) went to the city of Taif hoping to find people who would listen to, and support his message to humanity. Instead of support he found men, women and children who insulted and chased him out of town. With his sandals covered in blood and his heart full of sadness, he prayed to Allah for help.

In response, the Angel of the Mountains was sent down and he asked for the Prophet's permission to cause the mountains surrounding Taif to crumble, killing all of the city's inhabitants. Despite his pain and suffering, something he had every right to be angry about, the Prophet's (saws) reply was, "No, for I hope that Allah will bring forth from their progeny, people who will worship Allah Alone, and none besides Him."

Anger management in Islam can be summed up as follows.
- Seek refuge in Allah, from the tricks of Satan.
- Make ablution, because water extinguishes fire.
- Change positions, if you are standing, sit, if you are sitting, lie down.
    A person lying down cannot engage in fisticuffs or destroy property.
- Remove yourself from the situation. This could be likened to our
    modern equivalent, time out.

- Be silent, words spoken in anger cannot be taken back.

What Allah says about Using Intoxicants!

It has been claimed by many writers that the Arabic word "Khamr," which means (intoxicants like alcohol, and drugs) has not been completely prohibited in the Quran, but only discouraged. Others, mainly the followers of hadith, have claimed that alcohol has been prohibited in stages! The argument made here aims at presenting Quranic evidence that Allah prohibited the use of intoxicants, for getting intoxicated, and that this prohibition is immediate rather than being given in stages.

Allah says: "O Muhammad, say to them, "The things which my Lord has forbidden are: shameful deeds whether open or secret, sinful things and wrongdoing against the Truth. He has also forbidden to associate partners with Allah, since He has sent down no authority, therefore. (He has also forbidden) to attribute to Allah's name the thing which you know not He has said." [7 Al-A'raf:33]

The ban on intoxicants in the Quran is given through what is called syllogism. Syllogism is a form of reasoning where we have two given propositions called premises. When they are taken together they lead to a valid conclusion.

For example:
1- All men are mortal. (premise)
2- Muhammed is a man. (premise)
therefore:

3- Muhammed is mortal. (conclusion)

With regards to the ban on intoxicants in the Quran we read the following two premises:
1- (premise 1) Allah prohibited all 'ithm' the Arabic word for (sin). [7 Al- A'raf:33]

2- (premise 2) Allah says: They ask you about drinking and gambling, say, "In them are gross sins and benefits for the people, and their sinfulness is greater than their benefits." [2 Al-Baqarah:219]

3- Conclusion - Intoxicants, when used in any way which induces sin, as in getting drunk, or taking drugs to get high, is forbidden by Allah as all actions leading to sins are forbidden by Allah as in (premise 1).

Allah's disapproval of alcohol, and games of chance for betting is evident. In another verse the Muslims were prohibited from offering the Prayers when they were drunk. Finally drinking, gambling and the like were made absolutely unlawful.

In contrast, when intoxicants are used in any of the ways which provide benefits to mankind, without leading to sin, they are not forbidden. Examples of this type of use are the intoxicants used for medicine, for sterilization, for surgery, in anesthetics, etc. The words in Chapter 2 - Verse 219 which say that intoxicants have "benefits for the people" allow the use of intoxicants in these types of beneficial ways.

The Arabic word for sin is "ithm." Ithm literally means negligence. The sense of sin has entered into this word from 'athimah' which refers to a she-camel that can run fast, but willfully does not do so. Similarly, the man who neglects to obey the Commands of his Lord, in spite of his ability to do so, is considered to be sinful, for he has no intention of pleasing Allah.

It is such uses of intoxicants which contain (sin) that are forbidden. If intoxicants are used in surgery, or medicine it is clearly not spreading animosity, or hatred among people. It would, in fact, be helping people, and thus would not be forbidden.

The sinful ways of using intoxicants are further highlighted in the Quran in Chapter 5 - Verse 90, which tells us that intoxicants, and gambling are works of the devil. Also, in Chapter 5-Verse 91 where, we are told that the devil entices people to use intoxicants, and gambling to spread animosity and hatred between people, and to distract people from remembering Allah.

Allah says:
"Believers! Intoxicants, games of chance, idolatrous sacrifices at altars, and foreseeing by arrows are all extremely disliked. They are the handiwork of Satan. So turn wholly away from it that you may realize true success. By intoxicants, and games of chance, Satan desires to create enmity and hatred between you; and to turn you away from the remembrance of Allah, and from Prayer. Will you then, desist?" [5 Al-Maidah: 90-91]

Though the word khamr in Arabic literally means 'the drink made from grapes', it was also used figuratively, for intoxicating liquors made from wheat, barley, raisins, dates and honey. The Prophet (saws) applied the prohibition of wine to all intoxicants. In this regard we find statements from the Prophet (saws) found in the traditions, such as: "Every intoxicant is khamr, and every intoxicant is forbidden." "Every drink which causes intoxication is forbidden." "I forbid everything which intoxicates."

In a Friday sermon 'Umar defined khamr in the following manner: "Whatever takes hold of the mind is khamr." (Bukhari, Muslim, Ibn Majah)

The Prophet (saws) also clearly stated the following principle: "If anything causes intoxication when used in large quantity, even a small quantity of it is prohibited." "If a large quantity of something causes intoxication, to drink even a palmful of it is forbidden." (Abu Da'ud, Ibn Majah)

Allah says: "O Believers do not offer the Prayer while you are intoxicated. Prayer should only be offered, when you know what you are saying. Do not offer the Prayer if you are "unclean" until you take your bath, except when passing on the way. If you are sick or on a journey, or if any one of you has relieved himself, or you have touched women and can find no water, then cleanse yourselves with pure dust, by rubbing it on your face, and hands. No doubt Allah is Lenient and Forgiving." [4 An-Nisaa:43]

Some of the Muslims began to refrain from it from the first time. The majority of them, however, did not give it up, and often offered the Prayer in a state of intoxication, and made blunders in their recitations. This second Command came in the beginning of the year 4 A.H., and prohibited the offering of the Prayer while one was drunk. As a result they changed the timings of their drinking so as not to clash with the timings of the Prayers. Sometime after this, the Command for total prohibition as contained in [5 Al-Ma'idah: 90-91] was sent down.

The Arabic word sukarah (intoxicated) implies that this Command prohibits not only drinking, but every kind of intoxicant. Moreover, every intoxicating thing is in itself unlawful, the offense of intoxication becomes more heinous, when the Prayer is offered in, such a state. For the same reason, the Holy Prophet (saws) has instructed that when one feels sleepy, and dozes again and again during the Prayer, one should give up his Prayer and go to sleep.

Some people argue that the Prayer, from this verse, is no Prayer at all. Apart from the fact that it is an unnecessary hardship, the Arabic words of the Qur'an do not support this version. The Qur'an does not say, "unless you understand its meaning" or "unless you understand what you are saying" but it says "unless you know what you are saying". That means one should be in his senses to know what he is saying.

Some interpreters have referred to the words in Chapter 4 An-Nisaa:43 to claim that drinking alcohol is not forbidden by Allah. They explain that the words in 4:43 only forbid us from drinking alcohol at the time of the Prayer, which means that outside the times of the Prayer, drinking alcohol is allowed. It can be shown that this is a totally inaccurate interpretation of 4:43.

The words in 4:43 that say, "do not observe the Prayer while intoxicated" do not mean that using intoxicants is allowed by Allah outside the times for Prayer. These words simply tell us that intoxication deprives the believer from observing the Prayer.

In all the Quran, intoxication is the only sin that deprives the believer from observing the Prayer. If a person commits theft, adultery, or even murder, he/she should still observe his/her Prayer. This is because worshipping Allah is a duty on all believers, whether they commit sins or not. The case is different when a person is intoxicated. The reason for that is given in 4:43 by means of the words, "until you know what you are saying."

Under the effect of intoxication, a person does not know what he/she is saying, so it would be meaningless to pray to Allah in that state. This does not mean that using intoxicants is allowed by Allah outside of the time for Prayer.

In Chapter 5 - Verse 90 Allah says: "O you who believe, intoxicants, gambling, (ungodly) shrines and divining devices are afflictions that are the work of the devil. You shall 'ijtanibuhu' (stay away from him) so that you may succeed."

Some scholars have made referrence to this Verse, which speaks about intoxicants and other sins, and claimed that the Arabic word "ijtanibuhu", which as used in this verse means to avoid, or to stay away from intoxicants, and the other sins. That this word does not imply an absolute ban on intoxicants and the other sins.

However, an analysis of the Arabic words in 5:90 tells us that this is an inaccurate interpretation. The words that come before "ijtanibuhu" speak of 4 acts and not just intoxicants. The 4 acts are Intoxicants, Gambling, (ungodly) shrines and divining devices.

Those who make the case that intoxicants are discouraged, but not forbidden totally, do not mention the other 3 acts identified in the verse. They do not say that gambling, (ungodly) shrines and divining devices are merely discouraged. However, when we look at the word "ijtanibuhu", we note that it is in the singular and, that it follows the mention of the devil. Since it is in the singular, this word cannot refer to the 4 acts mentioned in the verse, because they are in the plural. It can only refer to a singular word. If the reference was to all 4 acts, the word to be used would have been 'ijtanibuhum' (stay away from them).

The word "ijtanibuhu" refers to the singular and it means to avoid him. This word refers to the singular noun which comes immediately before the word "ijtanibuhu", which is the devil. Allah is saying that these four acts are the work of the devil, and thus, you shall stay away from the devil. Further confirmation is given in the words that immediately follow, which continue to speak of the devil.

The devil only wants to provoke enmity, and hatred among, you through intoxicants and gambling, and to drive you away from remembering Allah, and from the Salat, so will you thus refrain? To conclude, the claim that alcoholic drinks are not strictly prohibited but only discouraged is a false claim.

Allah says: "(Likewise) We give you from date-palms and vines a drink from which you derive intoxicants, and also pure food. Indeed there is a Sign in this for those who make use of their common sense." [16 An-Nahl:67]

It is implied that the juice of the fruits of date-palms and vines contain two things. One is that which is pure and wholesome food for man, and the other is that which turns into alcohol after it becomes rotten. But it has been left to the choice of man to obtain pure healthy food from this providence, or to drink it as intoxicating wine to excite him, and make him lose his self-control. This also contains a hint as to the prohibition of wine that is to come.

Drinking alcohol was forbidden not only in the Quran, but also in previous Scriptures. In the Bible we read, in the King James Version:

"Wine is a mocker, strong drink a brawler; and whoever is led astray by it is not wise" (Proverbs 20:1).

30 They that tarry long at the wine; they that go to seek mixed wine. 31 Look not thou upon the wine when it is red, when it giveth his color in the cup, when it moveth itself aright. 32 At the last it biteth like a serpent, and stingeth like an adder. (Proverbs 23:30-32)

Before this last Command was given, the Holy Prophet (saws) addressed the people in order to prepare them for its absolute prohibition. He warned and said:

"Allah does not like at all that people should drink wine. Absolute forbiddance will soon be prescribed. Therefore, those who possess wine are advised to sell it." Some time after this, when verse 5:90 was sent down he declared: "Now those who possess wine, can neither drink it nor sell it. They should, therefore, throw it away."

Some people asked the Holy Prophet (saws): "May we convert it into vinegar?" He replied, "No, you must spill it."

Another asked again and again, "Is one permitted to use wine as medicine?" The Holy Prophet (saws) emphatically rejected this also and said, "No, it is not a medicine, but a disease."

Yet another asked, "Sir, we live in a place, which is very cold, and we have to do tiresome labor. So we drink wine to refresh ourselves from fatigue, and to keep warm in the cold." He asked, "Is what you drink an intoxicant?" The man replied, "Yes." The Holy Prophet (saws) replied, "Then refrain from it." At this the man said, "The people of our part of the country will not submit to this." He replied, "If they do not submit to this, then go to war with them."

According to a Tradition related by Umar, the Holy Prophet (saws) declared, "Allah has cursed wine, and the one who drinks it and the one who serves it and the one who sells it and the one who buys it, the one who extracts it, the one who has it extracted, the one who carried it and the one for whom it is carried."

During the time of the Holy Prophet (saws), there was no fixed punishment for a drunkard. The culprit, who was arrested and brought for trial, was beaten with shoes, kicked, given blows, and thrashed with sticks and ropes. Forty lashes were the maximum punishment given for this crime. The same was the punishment during the time of Abu Bakr, and the early days of Caliph Umar. When the latter saw that the crime was on the increase, he, in consultation with the other Companions, laid down eighty lashes for this.

Imam Malik and Imam Abu Hanifah and, according to a Tradition, Imam Shafi`i also, were of the same opinion. However, Imam Ahmad bin Hanbal and, according to another Tradition, Imam Shafi'i also, were of the opinion that forty lashes should be inflicted for the crime of drinking. Ali also considered forty lashes to be the punishment for it.

According to the Shari`ah, it is the duty of the Islamic State to enforce prohibition. That is why, during the time of Umar, the shop of a man who belonged to the clan of Bani-Thaqif, was burnt, by his order, because wine was secretly sold there. On another occasion a whole village was burnt down on the orders of Umar, for the crime that wine was secretly extracted and sold there.

Lightning Source UK Ltd.
Milton Keynes UK
UKHW010935061020
371099UK00001B/81